TEACHING MINORITIES MORE EFFECTIVELY

A Model For Educators

Thomas J. Brown

UNIVERSITY
PRESS OF
AMERICA

LANHAM • NEW YORK • LONDON

Copyright © 1986 by

University Press of America,® Inc.

4720 Boston Way
Lanham, MD 20706

3 Henrietta Street
London WC2E 8LU England

Library of Congress Cataloging in Publication Data

Brown, Thomas J., 1933-
    Teaching minorities more effectively.

    Bibliography: p.
    1. Minorities—Education—United States.
2. Teacher-student relationships—United States.
3. Motivation in education.   I. Title.
LC3731.B73   1986   371.97   86-18963
ISBN 0-8191-5662-0 (alk. paper)
ISBN 0-8191-5663-9 (pbk. : alk. paper)

All University Press of America books are produced on acid-free
paper which exceeds the minimum standards set by the National
Historical Publications and Records Commission.

To my family,

Joyce
Glynis
Daryl

ACKNOWLEDGEMENTS

My most sincere appreciation is being expressed to the following individuals for:

- Technical assistance provided by the staffs of Longfellow Elementary, Harper's Choice Middle, and Dunloggin Middle through the willingness of individual staff members to utilize various teaching strategies.

- Assistance in proofreading by my wife, Joyce.

- Typing of manuscript by Mrs. Joanne Parton and Mrs. Nancy Solomon.

CONTENTS

PREFACE

This handbook is designed to provide practical guidance for classroom teachers, supervisors, and administrators who are committed to achieving educational equity for minority students. The point of view reflected herein is that a scientific approach to the delivery of instructional services will result in conscious efforts to control or, at least, manipulate many of the variables which influence learning. While the ideas presented are limited in quantity and in scope, they are offered as access routes toward the alleviation of minority underachievement. If they accomplish no more than to arouse genuine interest on the one hand or to stimulate the desire to engage in critical self-analysis on the other, a useful purpose will have been served.

Thomas J. Brown

Columbia, Maryland
May, 1986

FOREWORD

There is and has been concern about the education of minority culture children in the U. S. The classroom pattern of "insist and resist" is prevalent when the culture of teachers and students is highly discrepant. This problem exists in a pronounced way for some minority children and their teachers. To the extent that teachers consciously design instruction to mute the power of this discrepancy, the students will want to learn and will be more capable of learning.

This handbook honors the contribution of teachers who are portrayed not as helpless bystanders, but as effective interventionists. They can, by conscious awareness and manipulation of cultural and instructional factors, facilitate the learning of minority culture students. By acknowledging the complex, interacting set of factors which makes up a classroom environment, the author further dignifies the teacher's role. Within this setting, teachers must examine premises, be aware of subtleties, see certain factors as having primacy, perceive situational necessities, and act skilfully.

Tom Brown, an educator with an extensive background of teaching minority students, has prescribed premise and technique which, when understood and utilized by teachers, will bond students and teachers together for the educational advantage of all students. The result will be an all-inclusive classroom for learning.

Frank T. Lyman, Jr.

Frank Lyman, a specialist in instructional technique and teacher education, is a Teacher Education Center Coordinator for the University of Maryland, College Park and Howard County Public Schools.

Chapter I

INTRODUCTION

Historical Perspective

When Jefferson proposed a system of public education over two hundred years ago, his expressed purpose was to eliminate the inequities brought about by the influence of political power and wealth on the private institutions. While the proposal did not allude to other discriminatory practices, one might assume that their alleviation was included in Jefferson's intent. What he probably did not foresee was the potential for schools governed by public officials and supported by public funds to operate in much the same manner and under many of the same influences as their private counterparts.

Historically, public education has been and continues to be controlled by members of the dominant culture in our society. It is a system whose major benefits accrue to white middle-class Americans. As such, the delivery of instructional services to and the learning outcomes for minority students reflect the many inequities the system continues to inflict upon them.

1

William Ryan, in <u>Blaming the Victim,</u> presents an eloquent indictment of public education's dysfunction for minorities. He writes:

> "We are dealing, it would seem, not so much with culturally deprived children as with culturally depriving schools. And the task to be accomplished is not to revise, and amend, and repair deficient children but to alter and transform the atmosphere and operations of the schools to which we commit these children. Only by changing the nature of the educational experience can we change its product. To continue to define the difficulty as inherent in the raw materials— the children—is plainly to blame the victim and to acquiese in the continuation of educational inequity in America."[1]

Throughout this writing, minorities are thought of as those who possess traits, characteristics, and other lifeways that run counter to those of the dominant culture. A scientific approach toward improving learning outcomes for these groups will be the focus for the discussions in the chapters that follow.

Effective Teaching

To define effective teaching in a manner which would hold universal appeal would be an extremely difficult task. Needless to say, it is a task which will not be undertaken at this time. The understanding that effective teaching involves input, process, and output variables interrelated in such a way that the absence of either renders it impotent is sufficient for this discussion. Many educators would agree that process variables comprise the critical component inasmuch as learning outcomes are determined to a large extent by their quality.

In an address before the general assembly of the Association of Teacher Educators, Asa Hilliard suggested that teaching effectiveness may be judged by comparing commonalities of processes used by our contemporaries with those employed by great teachers of the past. After identifying such figures as Socrates, Aesop, Jesus of Nazareth, and Paulo Freire as truly great teachers, he proceeded to point out that each took full advantage of the learners' existing knowledge.[2] Given what we know about the teaching-learning relationship, we can say that teaching effectiveness is a function of the teacher's skill in utilizing the learners' preexisting knowledge in bridging the gap between what they already know and what we are attempting to teach.

Whether teaching should be classified as an art, a science, or possibly neither could become the topic for a lively debate. There are some eminent educators whose philosophical posture would place them in either of those camps. However, an idea that should generate very little debate is that implicit in one's perception of teaching are suggestions regarding how it can be accomplished most effectively. It is this reality that serves as the catalyst for promoting the belief that teaching is indeed a science. To perceive it as an art is to place emphasis on its aesthetic appeal rather than its substance. While it is recognized that some teachers perform more artistically than others, it should be noted that substance rather than artistry is the critical attribute that determines relative effectiveness.

If we can accept the notion that learning is represented by changes in behavior and teaching is a process of interaction which facilitates learning,

3

then teaching can be thought of legitimately as a behavioral science. As such, it demands that all of the variables which influence learning be scientifically controlled or, at least, manipulated. When one perceives any pursuit as a science, implicit in that perception is the need for controlled interventions if maximum proficiency is desired. In the case of teaching, all of this can be accomplished in a manner which is pedagogically sound and aesthetically appealing.

While there is general agreement that effective teaching must be results contingent, there is little agreement on what the components ought to be. Thus, what may be judged effective teaching in one situation may be totally ineffective in another depending upon the desired results.

Some Issues Contributing to Minority Underachievement

The failure of many minorities to achieve academically is a well-documented reality. Irrefutable evidence of this fact has figured prominently in educational planning for the past twenty-five years. However, the rhetoric and the reforms, which also gained in popularity during that period, have resulted in relatively insignificant gains. Literally dozens of theories, many of which are supported by empirical research, have been advanced as explanations for the lack of academic achievement by Blacks, Hispanics, and Native Americans. Many of these theories suggest, by implication, that it is unreasonable to expect schools to help students rise above what are perceived as the educationally debilitating influences of minority lifeways. They provide a rationale for what is rather than a vision of what ought to be. The most disastrous result of all of this has been the reluctance of

4

educators to see the urgent need for making modifications to and refinements of what takes place in schools.

Educational equity is a term which is presently enjoying a high degree of visibility. Equity may be thought of as the outcome of efforts which eliminate disparity in results. When the term is applied to the delivery of instructional services, it suggests that learning outcomes commensurate with cognitive ability should ensue. Unfortunately, many educators continue to labor under the misapprehension which equates equity with equal access to educational opportunity. In reality, the two concepts are quite different. While equal access is a prerequisite for equity, it neither guarantees nor expedites its realization. The standard response by school districts across the country to demands for equity is the infusion of multi-cultural and multi-ethnic studies into the school curriculum. This emphasis has been looked upon as satisfying those demands and thus, effectively reducing any real sense of urgency for modifying the teaching process.

This discussion of issues contributing to minority underachievement cannot be concluded without mentioning the insidious effects of racism. So that these brief remarks will not be considered inflammatory, the concept of racism will be examined from a contemporary point of view which focuses only on power and oppression. This suggests that bigotry, discrimination, racial prejudice, and stereotyping could be eliminated entirely without changing the basic structures of the American way of life. When reduced to its essence, racism is the result of attempts to keep power, wealth, and control under the auspices of the dominant culture in our society. Since an important mission of

5

schooling is that of transmitting the culture, schools are, by definition, racist institutions.

Regardless of whether the ideas presented here can be embraced easily, it is clear that racism and many of the attitudes kindled by its philosophy can have a devastating effect on learning outcomes for racial and ethnic minorities. Those who share these attitudes must also share a large part of the responsibility for many continuing inequities.

Research tells us that teachers invariably form expectations about what students can achieve and how they will behave. These findings clearly demonstrate that teachers hold greater expectations for, pay more attention to, and assign higher grades to the performances of students who have been labeled high achievers, students who come from higher socio-economic stratas, and students who are white.[3]

Teachers are more likely to perceive minority students as low achievers. These perceptions are reflected through their interactions with these students and through their evaluations of student performances. In a study conducted by Crowl in 1971, sixty-two white teachers were asked to evaluate taped oral responses containing identically worded answers spoken by black and white ninth-grade boys. These teachers assigned significantly higher evaluations to recorded answers by white males. When black males gave objectively superior answers, those responses were given no higher evaluations than the inferior answers given by white boys.[4]

Similar studies have been replicated in different parts of the country and the results indicate that teachers, by acts of commission or omission,

6

continue to treat minorities inequitably. Because of the striking similarities in training, many of those teachers included in this indictment are themselves minority group members.

Critical Variable That Influence Learning

Reference was made earlier to the input, process, and output variables that are indigenous to the teaching-learning equation. Those variables, unlimited in number, exist in free variation depending upon the lesson objectives, the background and previous experiences of the learners, and the teacher's skill in exercising interactive behaviors that facilitate learning. The experiences gained from having taught for more than ten years in inner-city schools suggest to this writer that four of those variables emerge as critical in terms of their influences on education in general and on education for minorities in particular. These critical variables are:

Motivation
Classroom Behavior
Student/Teacher Interaction
Evaluation

In the chapters that follow, systematic approaches for controlling, or at least manipulating, those variables will be explored in some depth. While each will be treated separately for purposes of clarity, it should be understood that these variables are inextricable parts of a total process.

Chapter 1   FOOTNOTES

[1] William Ryan, <u>Blaming the Victim</u> (New York: Pantheon, 1971), p. 60.

[2] Ideas presented in the keynote address at the annual ATE conference by Asa Hilliard held in Orlando, Florida on January 29, 1983.

[3] Woodworth, W. P., and Salzer, R. T., "Black Children's Speech and Teacher Evaluations," <u>Urban Education</u> 6 (July, 1971), 167-173.

[4] Crowl, T. K., "White Teachers' Evaluation of Oral Responses Given by White and Negro Ninth Grade Males, "<u>Dissertation Abstracts</u> 3' (1971: 4540A.)

Chapter II

MOTIVATION

Motivation can be thought of as the general energizing syndrome that initiates, sustains and regulates various kinds of activity. While there are many conflicting theories concerning how it operates, the fact that it is a variable which affects learning enjoys universal agreement. Motivation can be used as a partial explanation for why some children excel academically while others with similar intellectual endowments underachieve. One definite conclusion that can be drawn is what might cause one individual or group to become highly motivated may have no observable influence on another.

Waetjen points out the popular misconception that if teachers make the curriculum content interesting by the use of a few audiovisual devices or by introducing excitement into the lesson, the students will be motivated to learn. He indicates that such assumptions serve to minimize efforts to accommodate individual differences as factors affecting learning rather than maximize them.[1]

For the discussion that follows, motivation will be separated into two components—interest and

9

transfer. These components, which have been arbitrarily derived, will be handled individually so that the importance of each may be emphasized.

Interest

There is little doubt that the interest for the learning task held by students exercises a controlling influence over both active and passive involvement in the educational exchanges that take place. However, the kind of interest referred to here is that which arises from perceptions of relevance and awareness of purpose for learning rather than the novelty of the experience. Needless to say, differences in culture and ethnicity among students suggest that while the same skills can be learned, they are learned for a variety of reasons.

The perceptive teacher recognizes immediately that the cultural diversity within the group for which the learning experience is planned dictates clearly the number of purposes which must be established. Multiple purposes are essential if relevance is to be perceived by each individual in the group. What happens all too often is that the purpose for learning is taken directly from a teachers' guide. Whatever relevance these statements may have pertains, almost exclusively, to middle-class white children.

It is precisely at this point in many lessons that the results of instructional inequities suffered by minorities begin to appear. Inattentiveness and eventually non-task oriented behaviors become the rule rather than the exception. Because of the teacher's failure to have students perceive the relevance of the learning experience at the very outset, many subsequent interactions are reduced to attempts at managing behavior. Multiply one incident by the number of minority students involved in any given lesson and the magnitude of the problem can be visualized clearly.

Many minorities, particularly Afro-Americans and Hispanics, are more easily motivated when the purpose for learning relates to needs which they perceive as real and immediate. Once those needs are recognized by the students, rapid movement from the introductory stage to the application stage is crucial if interest is to be sustained. They simply do not respond to purposes for learning which deal with future needs. By contrast, middle-class white students, whose achievement orientation begins early and is reinforced continuously by family lifestyles, respond to such purposes as preparation for college or scoring well on standardized tests. However, it is important to point out that this contrast is more a function of how culture influences cognition than it is a matter of being more or less motivated to achieve.

Despite considerable effort on the part of school districts across the country to bring cultural and ethnic relevance to the curriculum, there has not been a scientific approach toward manipulating those critical variables that make the difference between success or failure in implementation. Conventional assumptions which suggest that there are a number of strategies which can be used to motivate all children regardless of their culture is another example of how minority students are victimized by the system.

David Finley, in an article entitled, "Why Eskimo Education Isn't Working," gives his assessment of education's struggle for survival in the community of Wainwright, Alaska. He concludes that significant educational progress eludes them for two basic reasons. He cites as those reasons the turmoil created by a culture in transition and the fact that Wainwright exists in complete isolation from the mainstream of Alaskan society. Finley goes on to point out that the village of Wainwright is the only world these children have known. To counteract this, the district superintendent has ordered teachers to individualize instruction to meet students' special needs. However, a major problem created by that endeavor results from the discrepancy between what the school and what the students perceive those needs to be. The fact that students do not see themselves as needing what the school has to offer is clearly reflected through low achievement.[2]

A similar situation exists in those schools located on reservations for Native Americans. This fact is pointed out dramatically by the failure of Title IV programs to raise achievement levels of the students involved. Whether one accepts the implied analogy between lifestyles on reservations and those indigenous to other minority groups throughout the country, the fact that some similarities exist should be readily conceivable. Prominent among those similarities is the ever-present conflict between what curriculum designers and program consumers perceive as educational needs. It is recognized that the mismatch between curriculum offerings and what students perceive as their needs creates a major challenge for the teacher. Until such time that curriculum modifications are made, our efforts should be directed toward creating learning experiences which hold meaningful purposes for all children.

How teachers perceive individual students' general state of motivation is reflected through the expectations held for their academic performance. Because minority students may not respond enthusiastically to many of the learning tasks they confront, the attribute most often thought to be responsible is lack of motivation. These misguided assumptions of lack of motivation combine with low expectations for academic achievement to form insurmountable obstacles for these groups. Our share toward removing these obstacles should be:

1. A commitment to provide minority students with the skills they need to experience success in school.

2. An awareness that each successive approximation of what students are capable of accomplishing should be reinforced.

3. An adequate understanding of and appreciation for minority cultures.

There is no easy way for teachers to acquire that set of understandings nor is there an acceptable alternative for its acquisition.

Creating Interest

Interest, as it is being used here, emanates from students' perceived relevance of the learning experience. The scenarios that follow should indicate its importance to the teaching/learning equation. An introduction to division of common fractions is being used for this illustration simply because it is considered by many educators to be the most difficult concept taught at the elementary level.

13

Typically, the standard approach followed in an introductory lesson would include some discussion of the purpose of the unit of study, how the skills included will relate to those taught in the previous units, and how information gained through this unit will be instrumental in promoting understanding of the units which will follow. Only on rare occasions will teachers attempt to have students realize the immediate impact of learning outcomes. On those occasions when this is attempted, those efforts usually consist of making the students aware of the influence of their performance on standardized test scores and grades. This entire process might consume from 15 to 20 minutes of the period.

It is conceivable that the procedure outlined above might stimulate sufficient levels of interest so that all of the students would become highly motivated to achieve. However, that is not usually the case. Most of the minority students would be left with perceptions of irrelevance and lack of enthusiasm for what the unit has to offer. When these kinds of perceptions are formed at the very outset of any learning experience, student involvement progresses through all the stages from disinterest to disruptive behavior. All of this gets translated into national statistics which reflect for minorities: (1) Lack of academic achievement; (2) Reduced teacher expectations for academic performance; (3) A high percentage of student suspensions; (4) A high percentage of student dropouts; and (5) An inordinately large percentage of students being labeled learning disabled.

Now let's analyze another scenario which, at least, holds forth the promise of stimulating perceptions of relevance by all of the students in the class. Introductory discussions should establish

14

clearly that regardless of who we are, where we live, to what values we subscribe, and how we manage our lifestyles, divisions of fractions have significant effects on the lives of all of us. Emphasis should be placed on the notion that while many of us are affected in different ways, the results are no less important. This discussion should include specific examples of how the division of fractions may be used in ways peculiar to the various groups represented. More importantly, each individual should be led to the realization that one's quality of life is diminished somewhat by a lack of understanding of division of fractions and its uses. Evolving from these types of educational exchanges are clear student perceptions of purposes which are relevant, and clear teacher perceptions of how the new unit can be related to the students' extemporaneous knowledge base.

It should be obvious that the process being described here cannot be handled successfully in a 15 or 20-minute time periods. Depending upon the amount of cultural, ethnic, and economic diversity present, this process can consume as much as three hours of instructional time. However, if the three hours, or whatever amount of time, required to ensure that relevance is perceived by all of the students in the class is invested up front, the amount of instructional time relegated to managing behavior is reduced significantly. The choice for teachers is whether to invest the time on the front end or to risk the loss of substantially more instructional time in dealing with non-task oriented behaviors.

While these introductory discussions are orchestrated by teachers, the ideas, experiences, analogies, and questions are all student generated. Students bring to school memories, experiences, knowledge, concerns, and some curiosity which can relate in some way to any aspect of the school curriculum imaginable. It is through this open educational exchange that we are made aware of how certain learning experiences impact on their lives. To encourage student participation in that process, teachers should establish clearly that:

1. Regardless of racial or ethnic identity and economic status, the unit about to be taught affects the lives of all of us.

2. While many of us are affected in different ways, the results are no less important.

3. Specific concepts and their uses are peculiar to various cultural groups.

4. One's very existence is diminished somewhat by a lack of understanding of the concepts presented and the variety of ways in which they are utilized.

Facilitating Transfer

In this monograph, the term transfer is used to describe a process of bridging between what students already know and what they are attempting to learn. This should suggest that the relationships established between students' existing knowledge base and the new learning task have a tremendous influence on the time requirements for skills acquisition. There is an abundance of clinical evidence that indicates the degree of difficulty associated with the teaching of any skill is directly related to the degree of success achieved in creating perceptions of relevance and establishing positive transfer.

An example of how positive transfer may be established in teaching the division of fractions will be used for the purpose of illustration. The first step in this process is to determine what prerequisite skills students must possess if an adequate understanding of the process is to be acquired. The critical prerequisite concepts for understanding the division of fractions are:

1. Identity Element for Division: The identity element for division is (1). By definition, it is that number which, when used as a divisor, produces a quotient identical to the dividend.

Examples:

$$1\overline{)12}^{\,12} \quad \text{or} \quad 1\overline{)13}^{\,13} \quad \text{or} \quad 1\overline{)17}^{\,17}$$

2. The Law of Reciprocals: This law states that any number multiplied by its reciprocal equals one (1). A reciprocal is the inverted form of a number.

Examples: The reciprocal of 2 is 1/2; the reciprocal of 1 is 1/1; the reciprocal of 1/7 is 7/1 etc.

$$2/1 \times 1/2 = 2/2 = 1$$

$$1/1 \times 1/1 = 1/1 = 1$$

$$1/7 \times 7/1 = 7/7 = 1/1$$

3. The Principle of Compensation for Division: This principle states that both the divisor and dividend may be multiplied or

divided by the same number without changing the quotient.

Examples:

$$\overset{2}{2\overline{\smash{)}4}} \quad \text{or} \quad 6\left(\overset{2}{2\overline{\smash{)}4}}\right) = \overset{2}{12\overline{\smash{)}24}} \quad \text{or} \quad \frac{\overset{2}{2\overline{\smash{)}4}}}{2} = \overset{2}{1\overline{\smash{)}2}}$$

The second step in the process is to teach any of these critical prerequisite concepts which the students do not already possess.

The third and final part of this process is to create a strategy for teaching the division of fractions that will relate this new skill to some previously acquired knowledge. An initial step in this phase might be to change the graphic representation of the examples from the way they are usually presented in textbooks to a less threatening form.

Example:

$$\text{Change } \frac{1}{2} \div \frac{1}{4} \quad \text{to} \quad \frac{1}{4}\overline{\smash{)}\frac{1}{2}}$$

The rationale for making this kind of change is because the students are already familiar with the standard division algorithm. Our goal is to take full advantage of what they already know. Working with the example, $1/4 \div 1/2$, you might ask the students what number used as a divisor makes the operation of division easiest to perform. They will remember that the identity element for division is one (1). They should also remember that any number multiplied by its reciprocal equals one (1). After performing that operation, our example now looks like this.

$$\frac{4}{1} \times \frac{1}{4} = \frac{4}{4} = 1\overline{\smash{\big)}\ \frac{1}{2}}$$

Now they must use the principle of compensation which they have already learned. This principle reminds them that since the divisor was multiplied by the reciprocal of 1/4 which is 4/1, the dividend must be multiplied by the same number. Now our example appears this way:

$$\frac{4}{1} \times \frac{1}{4} = \frac{4}{4} = 1\overline{\smash{\big)}\ \frac{4}{1} \times \frac{1}{2} = \frac{4}{2} = 2} \quad \text{or} \quad 1\overline{\smash{\big)}\ 2}^{\,2}$$

At this step in the process, the students recognize that they are performing a new operation by utilizing skills and concepts which have been learned previously. Not only can they perform the operation of dividing fractions successfully, but more importantly, they understand each step of the process. Similar kinds of strategies can be used to teach any skills desired. The key to success is to utilize what students already know. When this is accomplished effectively, students can and will learn whatever we choose to teach them. What is most distressing about the lack of achievement by minorities is the fact that its major contributing factor is ineffective teaching.

1   Karl Waetjen, Comments made in an address before a symposium on education in Chicago in 1978.

2   D. Finley, "Why Eskimo Education Isn't Working," <u>Phi Delta Kappan</u>, LXIV (April, 1983), 580-581.

Chapter III

CLASSROOM BEHAVIOR

Another critical variable that influences learning is classroom behavior. When viewed as one of those variables that can be controlled, it takes on added significance because of its far-reaching impact. More specifically, displays of disruptive behavior as well as teacher attempts at maintaining control impede learning not only for the participants but also for the witnesses. In general, teachers receive some training in the principles of behavior management, but far too many are ill-equipped to deal effectively with behaviors that represent conflicts between what is expected at school and what is accepted in the home and the community.

The correlation between time on task and learning has been thoroughly documented by many empirical studies. This has resulted in the advancement of many accepted techniques for encouraging on-task behavior. However, to suggest that by employing the many excellent strategies which have been devised, non-task oriented behavior will be non-existent is a gross misrepresentation of classroom reality. The problem, particularly as it relates to minorities and how their behavior is perceived and reacted to by teachers, is more complex than it may appear.

In a study of the twenty-one largest school districts in the country, one researcher found that 72% of all student suspensions was black. Black students are not only suspended more frequently, but their suspensions are also for longer periods of time and less serious offenses than their white peers.[1]

As behavioral scientists, we have an obligation to examine all of the factors that influence behavior. This becomes even more crucial with the realization that many of the expectations held by teachers for student/teacher and student/student interactions set up real culture conflicts for minority children. Janice Hale points out that these conflicts are never resolved. Neither the school's expectations nor the influence of the child's culture is likely to change.[2]

However, what can change, when encouraged in an atmosphere of mutual respect, is the child's desire to conform to the rules. That atmosphere of mutual respect is engendered when teachers seek information about minority cultures from all available sources, verify the information obtained to form a knowledge base, and develop from that knowledge base a set of understandings which modifies their own behavior.

Managing behavior becomes a problem only when the time and energy required to establish positive attitudes toward learning have not been invested. The chances of problems developing are minimized when teachers (1) create interest in the learning activity by having children perceive its relevance and (2) establish positive transfer by relating the new learning to things which the students already know. Since there are no guarantees that these two lesson components will be satisfied for each child, effective behavior management techniques must be addressed.

It is clear that the conventional wisdom upon which many teachers have come to rely for dealing with disruptive behavior is functionally obsolete. That obsolescence was brought on by the increases in cultural and ethnic diversity in many classroom settings. The need for developing a set of understandings regarding minority cultures should be underscored. Those understandings will emerge as constant reminders that our purpose for controlling behavior is to facilitate interactions that enhance learning. That purpose is best served when we encourage students to make appropriate choices based on a range of consequences. Because mutual respect is often destroyed by teacher acts of commission rather than acts of omissions, emphasis will be placed on things which should not be done.

Don't Moralize

Moralizing about inappropriate behavior should be left to parents, nuns, and members of the clergy. When teachers engage in this practice, they run the risk of destroying mutual respect and jeopardizing the prospects for subsequent meaningful interactions. Moralizing is the equivalent of passing judgment on behaviors as well as those who exhibit them. Implicit in the characterization of a given behavior as wrong or bad is a subtle indictment of those who display it. Because many of those behaviors are supported by family life styles and exhibited by parents, other relatives, and friends, any allegations of moral decay are directed toward an entire social structure. When examined

23

from this point of view, the problems created by moralizing are brought more clearly into focus. A single encounter of this nature creates obstacles to productive interaction which are extremely difficult to overcome.

Don't Demean Behaviors

The practice of demeaning behaviors differs from moralizing in two respects. There is a conscious effort made to separate the offense from the offender, and to avoid the issue of right or wrong. However, the behavior is described in such demeaning terms as uncouth, disgusting, immoral, repulsive, etc. For many of the same reasons that apply to moralizing, the results of demeaning behaviors are also disastrous in terms of how subsequent interactions are affected. IF WE CAN'T INTERACT WITH STUDENTS, WE CAN'T TEACH THEM.

Don't Get Into Power Struggles

For teachers and administrators to give the impression that they possess the power to force students to comply with their wishes and demands is to invite defiance. The right to exercise freedom of choice is one that all humans cherish. To suggest that a right so precious should be denied to students solicits rebellion. We do not diminish ourselves by admitting openly that we cannot make students do anything. A more reasonable approach is to explain rules, expectations, and the range of consequences for nonconformance. This approach encourages students to make appropriate choices while at the same time it affirms their right to choose.

Don't Ignore Inappropriate Behavior

The point of view being advanced here is that there are no educationally sound purposes served by ignoring unacceptable behaviors. It is a questionable practice, at best, which confuses the issue regarding what behaviors will and what behaviors will not be accepted by teachers. Since the challenging of limits by some students is predictable, clearly defined boundaries eliminate many displays of testing behaviors.

It is important to understand that most nonconforming behavior does not follow from students' desires to disregard school rules and regulations, but rather from the social structures from which reinforcement is derived. Teachers who can accept that fact direct their energies toward encouraging youth to make appropriate choices. Those who persist in defining classroom management as a campaign to eradicate those behaviors that assault their personal values are not only fighting a losing battle, they are erecting barriers that help render the primary mission of schooling ineffective.

The case scenarios that follow are intended to illustrate how the guiding principles discussed may be utilized in various situations.

Situation #1 Stealing

A conference needs to be held with a student and her parents regarding the student's involvement in the theft of a teacher's purse. The student was observed running from the classroom with the purse in her hand. Conversation between the stu-

25

dent involved and the teacher who observed the incident revealed that the student felt no remorse for what she had done. In fact, she presented what she perceived to be adequate justification for stealing. What kinds of things should be covered in the conference?

Guiding Principles to Follow

Dealing with those guilty of stealing requires a conscious effort to resist the temptation to characterize that behavior as morally wrong. No matter how persuasive our own beliefs, there are those who, without reservation, present some rather interesting justifications for committing thefts. Whether or not we can accept those justifications should not close our minds to the fact that some people do. For those people, the values to which they subscribe form the basis for many real-life decisions. Values are neither right nor wrong; they simply exist in all of us. In consideration of these facts, conferences should deal with the results of stealing and the range of consequences it attracts such as:

1. It results in the victim's loss of personal property.

2. It is a violation of the victim's civil and property rights.

3. It decreases motivation to strive for legitimate gains.

4. Having been found guilty places one in the position of becoming a prime suspect in subsequent thefts.

5. There is a range of consequences those guilty of stealing may suffer.

If you handle stealing without moralizing or demeaning the act, you are likely to avoid those pitfalls when dealing with any kinds of inappropriate behavior encountered.

Situation #2 Fighting

In an inner-city high school, which has no formal dress code, a fight erupted between a Jewish boy and another student of German descent who was wearing a tee shirt bearing an emblem of Nazi Germany and a derogatory remark directed toward the Jewish population in general. What kinds of things should be dealt with in separate conferences with each boy and his parents?

Guiding Principles to Follow

Unlike other culture conflicts which arise from behaviors that are affirmed by various social structures but are inappropriate for school, fighting presents a special kind of dilemma for many students. This is particularly true for those who are told by their parents that under no circumstances are they to suffer any physical abuse without retaliating. Because of these parental expectations, the choice of whether to fight and suffer the consequences or whether to conform to school rules is no longer a matter of student discretion. As a result, many youth who may be committed to peaceful means of conflict resolution feel honor bound to fight. Teachers and administrators who intervene in these kinds of situations need to exhibit genuine sensitivity for the no-win position of those children.

In handling the conference with students who have engaged in fighting, it is important to remind them of your expectations for their behavior and the range of consequences that applies for nonconformance. Of equal importance is the need to have students understand that the school's position against fighting and the parents' demands that they fight under certain conditions are attempts to accomplish the same thing. The safety of students and the protection of their civil rights are the motivating forces in both instances. You can sympathize with students and still invoke whatever consequences you deem appropriate. By avoiding demeaning the behavior and criticizing the parents for demanding displays of physical violence, you have not damaged the chances for subsequent meaningful interactions with either.

Situation #3 Profane Language

On a number of separate occasions, students have reported the use of profanity by several black children in your school cafeteria. When confronted with these charges in the privacy of your office, profanity was used by one of these students while attempting to explain the provocation for the other instances. What things need to be emphasized in the conference?

Guiding Principles to Follow

Teachers should understand that in many Afro-American subcultures, cursing is recognized as an art form. It is something that many people who are indigenous to those cultures do with pride. It is not uncommon for one to inquire about another's state of health by asking, "How the hell are yah?"

28

Friendly competition in creative cursing is thought to be not only relaxing, but to have some therapeutic value. If awards were offered in recognition of this kind of achievement, they would be dominated by Blacks. Prominant displays of this "performing art" may be heard in any part of the country where influences of Afro-American culture exist.

Regardless of its prominence as a part of the cultural heritage of Blacks, those who insist upon cursing in schools usually face some kind of reprimand. A key point for consideration is that it should be neither tolerated nor demeaned, but handled in a manner which encourages the use of vocabulary that is appropriate for the school setting. One way to accomplish this successfully is to deal with the student privately. Let him or her know that occasionally we all use language that is not appropriate for a given set of circumstances. Explain your awareness of the use of profanity in many popular movies, on television, in the community, and in many homes. At the same time, emphasize the fact that it is inappropriate for school. Remember, don't moralize with children. The minute they perceive anything you say as an attack on their morality as well as the moral fiber of other family members, the kind of relationship that must exist for meaningful interactions to occur has suffered a severe setback.

The purpose for controlling behavior cannot be overemphasized. It is done to facilitate interactions that enhance learning. If that purpose is lost, all of our efforts will be counterproductive.

[1] L. Hall, "Race and Suspension; A Second General Desegregation Problem," In Moody, C.D., William, J., and Vergen, C.B. (eds.), <u>Student Rights and Discipline</u>. Ann Arbor, Michigan: University of Michigan, School of Education, 1978.

[2] Ibid.

[3] Janice E. Hale, <u>Black Children: Their Roots, Culture and Learning Styles</u>, New York: Brigham, 1982, p. 36.

Chapter IV

STUDENT/TEACHER INTERACTION

Teaching, when reduced to its essence, may be thought of as interaction that induces learning. While learning can occur without the benefit of teaching, such learning is relatively inconsequential in terms of producing an educated citizenry. The more contemporary view of the educative process reflects the belief that its success or failure rests on the quality of the teaching involved therein. If one accepts the notion that the quality of teaching is tied to the quality of the interaction between students and teachers, then the importance of controlling, or at least manipulating, these interactions becomes crucial. The exchanges, both verbal and nonverbal, that take place in the classroom are predicated on communication. How the communication process facilitates the transformation of isolated exchanges into meaningful interaction can be measured along two dimensions. Those dimensions are the influence of teacher expectations on interaction patterns and the influence of students' language facility on teacher behaviors.

Influence of Teacher Expectations on Interaction Patterns

Few areas of the teaching/learning process have

been investigated more thoroughly than that of classroom interaction patterns. Prominent among these investigations are the efforts of Leacock, 1969; Brophy and Good, 1974; Braun, 1976; Cooper, 1977; Terman, 1979; and Good, 1981. The preponderance of that research suggests that students for whom low expectations for academic achievement are held are taught less effectively than those for whom teachers hold high expectations. In general, students who are not expected to make significant progress experience limited opportunities to engage actively in learning activities. Teachers are less likely to plan for or direct instruction toward this group. These students, most of whom are minorities, come under fewer teacher demands for academic performance and increasingly greater demands for conformance in terms of behavior.

The literature on teacher and school effectiveness has established clearly the existence of a causal relationship between teacher expectations and student achievement. Good suggests that every research effort that has examined this relationship serves to confirm that conclusion.[1] This causal relationship theory has prompted some researchers to question which phenomenon is the cause and which is the result. They suggest that it would be as logical to maintain that prior achievement influences teacher expectations as it would be to argue the reverse. However, that debate has very little relevance to this discussion. The position being presented here is that teachers have a moral, if not a legal, obligation to hold high expectations for all students regardless of prior achievement or ethnic background.

There is a growing research base which indicates that teacher expectations and the behaviors that accompany those expectations do significantly more than merely sustain differences among achievement levels. Brattesani, et al., found that in classrooms where students perceived differential treatment of low and high achievers, 9 to 18 percent of the variance in achievement levels was attributed to teacher expectations which were not based on a knowledge of prior accomplishments. Their findings were consistent with the belief that teachers interact with children in ways that communicate their expectations for individual student performances. More specifically, they indicate that although these expectations may deviate from children's prior performances, present performance is influenced significantly by their impact.[2]

Several summary statements which can be extracted from this body of research are the following:

1. Teachers hold greater expectations for, pay more attention to, and assign higher grades to the performances of students who have been labeled high achievers, students who come from higher socio-economic backgrounds, and students who are white.

2. Teacher expectations along with the behaviors that accompany them can produce achievement variations among children with similar intellectual endowments. This is true regardless of whether the expectations are based on prior performance or teacher assumptions about what students can achieve.

3. Teacher expectations serve to sustain pre-existing achievement differences

among children as they progress through school.

4. Teacher expectations which are inconsistent with children's prior performances can bring about changes in subsequent levels of achievement.

The self-fulfilling prophecy theory which suggests that children who perceive themselves as low achievers perform accordingly, does not address the differential kinds of treatment these students receive. The simple fact is that those for whom low expectations are held are taught in a manner which hardly could produce anything else.

These variables, teacher expectations and the kinds of teacher behaviors that either support or are supported by them, are under the complete control of those responsible for delivering instructional services. The fact that many teachers allow these variables to operate in ways that limit academic growth for some students can be attributed to an affinity for intuitive teaching. As was pointed out in an earlier discussion, this kind of teaching precludes those who utilize it from engaging in critical self-analyses of their teaching behaviors.

It is reasonable to assume that many teachers, who suppress achievement through their interactive behaviors with youth, do so unwittingly. However, what happens to the victims is a huge price for them to pay for the lack of teacher awareness. This would seem to strengthen the case for encouraging conscious-level teaching. The following scenarios are provided to sharpen the contrast between that approach and intuitive teaching and the relative benefits of each.

Teachers intuitively attempt to reinforce acceptable and encourage remediation of unacceptable behaviors by using statements of praise or statements designed to point up inadequacies. Such statements as, "I like the fact that you are whispering," or "Please lower your voices," can be heard in classrooms throughout the country. While such statements are effective in encouraging the behaviors desired, they are usually divorced from academic goals. This practice reinforces student perceptions that what pleases teachers most is good behavior. Stated differently, students perceive behavior rather than learning as the most important part of the mission of schooling.

By contrast, consciously determined statements such as, "I like the fact that you are working quietly," or "Please lower your voices so the work of this group won't be disturbed," emphasize how appropriate behavior enhances the learning environment. While the differences may appear to be subtle, the impact on students is significant. A thorough analysis of how various statements, strategies, and other forms of interaction influence learning is the hallmark of conscious-level teaching.

It is also important to contrast the two approaches with regard to the impact of each on specific academic outcomes. For purposes of bringing that contrast more clearly into focus, a teacher behavior associated with each approach will be examined.

Let us assume that students in two separate 4th grade classes were asked by their teachers to write a paragraph about a recent experience. Although both classes have had some developmental lessons on experience writing, this assignment represented their first attempt at writing a paragraph independently. The students of both classes were anxious to know what length their paragraphs should be. The intuitive response from one teacher suggested that approximately 1/2 page would be acceptable. The consciously determined response from the other teacher suggested that 8 to 12 sentences would be acceptable.

Since students of this age group often conceptualize paragraphs in terms of length rather than as units of meaning with interrelated components, efforts to produce them can result in run-on sentences, fragments, and disregard for the use of capital letters and end marks of punctuation. Finished products of this quality are typical when students are preoccupied primarily with the amount of writing they have to do. However, the other teacher's consciously determined response suggesting a range of between 8 and 12 sentences forced students to focus on the sentence. This focus alone served to eliminate many of the problems described above. As was mentioned earlier, the subtle difference between the two approaches can have a tremendous impact on student achievement.

Ironically, intuitive teaching has been accorded a certain amount of prestige which increases the difficulty of promoting conscious-level teaching. Principals, supervisors, department heads, and resource teachers who recognize the need to keep abreast of innovative practices often walk into classrooms and begin teaching. These performances are displays of intuitive teaching in its purest form. The learning outcomes produced by some of these impromptu teaching stints are commendable. However, they are significantly less than they might have been had consciously determined interactions been employed.

Most educators would agree that those who occupy positions of leadership ought to reserve some time for teaching. There is no more practical way to stay in touch with the realities of classroom life. What should be kept in mind is that each time demonstration lessons are taught, those teaching are modeling behaviors that, presumably, should be encouraged in others. The extent to which this modeling reinforces behaviors that should be extinguished is exactly the extent to which a practice can be invaluable on the one hand and counterproductive on the other.

Influence of Students' Language Facility on Teacher Behaviors

One of the major premises on which the philosophy of culturally pluralistic education rests is the belief that differences should not only be tolerated, they should be affirmed. Nothing violates that principle more flagrantly than those strategies for delivering instructional services which embrace the concepts of "nonstandard or substandard English."

The discussion that follows should not be perceived as one which minimizes the obligation of teachers to promote student facility with the prestige dialect, but rather one which emphasizes how increased sensitivity toward the use of dialectical variants can enhance student/teacher interactions.

The key to successful communication is mutual intelligibility. Those who have increased their own understanding of and tolerance for urban ghetto speech have enhanced the communication process between their students and themselves. It is important for all of us, particularly those who have the responsibility for guiding the learning experiences of inner-city children, to recognize the legitimacy of the many dialects of American English and to utilize those dialects in establishing access routes to more effective communication. Those educators who are willing to accept the notion that English grammar is descriptive as opposed to prescriptive in that it sets forth the language as it is rather than as it ought to be, perceive the existence of a grammar for each of the various dialects. Comparative studies and progressive differentiations between those dialects and the prestige dialect result in:

1. Establishing the idea that languages, regardless of the number of dialects in existence, are systematic.

2. Providing native speakers of variant dialects with a frame of reference which facilitates their ability to switch codes from one dialect to another.

3. Promoting the understanding that a given dialect may be more appropriately used for certain occasions than for some other.

Children whose basic speech patterns are comprised of dialectical variants are often reluctant to offer oral contributions to classroom activities. This is particularly true if they have good reason to believe that those contributions will be judged for their conformance with accepted language conventions rather than content. Reticence on the part of these students elicits teacher interactions which serve to exacerbate further an already dehumanizing experience. The students soon succumb to feelings of not belonging and withdraw completely from all learning activities. This may be thought of as the point of no return. Regardless of teacher efforts to get these children actively involved, the forces operating against meaningful interaction are too firmly entrenched. Predictably, the outcomes of these actions and reactions are the same. Another group of minority students continues to make only marginal progress over the course of the school year.

What has just been described is a sad scenario that occurs with alarming regularity. But it occurs because well-meaning teachers are perceived by students as the source of their humiliation. They react to teachers by finding subtle ways to convey the message, "I CAN'T TALK TO YOU FOOL; WE DON'T SPEAK THE SAME LANGUAGE." The saddest commentary of all is that this can be avoided. The discussion that follows provides a conceptual framework for utilizing knowledge considered by many to be academically limiting.

Many educators need to be reminded that teaching is much more than merely presenting information. It is a process of human interaction predicated on communication which induces learning. Interaction and communication form the very essence of the process. When either of those essentials is lacking, the process is doomed to failure. This is precisely what happens when teachers feel the need for having every statement made by students conform to spoken language conventions. An option which makes more sense involves utilizing what students already know in teaching what we want them to learn.

Obviously, the chances of finding written grammars for any of the variant dialects of American English are remote. However, writing a grammar can be accomplished simply by collecting and analyzing samples of children's speech patterns. School playgrounds, cafeterias, and field trips provide ideal settings through which a fairly inclusive sampling can be obtained. It is essential that the speech samples collected be distributed among all of the tenses utilized in the dialect under study. Structuring casual conversation to elicit certain types of responses is one way to ensure that this has been accomplished.

The procedure described above revealed the following information about a typical variant dialect:

1. This particular dialect utilized only five tenses (Future, Habitual, Present, Past, and Past Participle).

2. A contraction of be and is (be's) is voiced consistently in habitual tense verb forms.

3. The pure verb is omitted in the present tense.

4. Done is used as an auxiliary in the past tense.

5. Been done is used to form the variant counterpart for the past participle.

6. Gunna is always used to form the future tense.

Examples:

Habitual Tense......... He be's running.
Present Tense......... She running.
Past Tense .... He done ran.
Past Participle .... She been done ran.
Future Tense.......... He gunna run.

These are the only tenses employed in this dialect, and they are used consistently in the same manner. Most native speakers of any dialect understand it thoroughly and speak it fluently. There are many of these variant dialects of American English which conform to neither the writing nor the speaking conventions of the prestige dialect. However, their legitimacy rests on the following facts:

1. They are systematic.

2. They satisfy the requirement of mutual intelligibility.

3. They are important aspects of specific cultures.

To perceive them as "substandard" or "non-standard" is to condescend, while to share such perceptions with native speakers is criminal.

Working with variant dialects may become a painful experience for some educators. In spite of the pain which may accompany this exercise, it is an investment of time and energy that can pay huge dividends. Teachers who are willing to make this investment are perceived by their students as caring and sincere individuals who can relate to them in a number of ways. They perceive teacher expectations for their academic achievement to be high, and they respond to those expectations enthusiastically. Through this approach, children who speak urban ghetto speech can be taught to acquire and to use the prestige dialect in a relatively short period of time. More importantly, this process helps to establish a learning environment that reflects mutual respect. Although the educational outcomes produced are incredible, the strategy holds no special magic. It is an example of effective teaching enhanced by consciously determined educational exchanges with youth. If minority underachievement is to be eliminated, their culture and ethnicity will figure prominantly in the process.

Chapter 4   Footnotes

[1] T. L. Good, "Teacher Expectations and Student Perceptions: A Decade of Research," <u>Educational Leadership</u> 38 (April, 1981), 415-422.

[2] Brattesani, et al., <u>Motivation and Achievement</u>, New York: Wiley, 1974, p. 179.

Chapter V

EVALUATION

The concept of evaluation formed by many teachers, particularly those with less than five years of experience, often relates exclusively to the assignment of grades to papers, projects, tests, and progress reports. However, teachers are afforded many more opportunities to assess, praise, and criticize students' work verbally. Those comments, which range from superlatives to diminutives, are influential in shaping students' perceptions of their intellectual strengths and weaknesses. This chapter will focus on an array of teacher behaviors which serves to change the process of evaluation into one of devaluation.

Just as teacher expectations affect student achievement, their influence on how that achievement is evaluated is equally profound. Whether that influence is transmitted directly through grades or written comments assessing the quality and quantity of work produced or indirectly through accepting or rejecting students' responses, the results can be devastating to minority students. Because of the research done on teacher expectations and student achievement, much of which has been cited previously, the fact that a discernible

45

relationship exists is well established. Although the debate surrounding which is the cause and which is the effect continues, the evidence is heavily weighted toward the identification of teacher expectations influencing rather than being influenced by student achievement.

One of the more serious indictments against evaluation is that it often reflects teacher perceptions of student behavior as well as achievement. This observation is supported by the fact that boys usually score higher than girls on tests of math and science yet girls receive better grades in these same subjects on report cards. Evaluation of minority students' work suffers even greater contamination because these children behave in ways that are different from middle-class white students. Teachers see that atypical behavior not only as unacceptable but limiting in terms of academic growth.

The discussion on behavior in Chapter III points out the fact that far too many teachers are ill-equipped to deal effectively with behaviors which present disruptions to normal classroom routines. Teacher frustrations arising from feelings of not being in control are vented through the process of evaluating student achievement. The grade book becomes a smoking gun. As a result, the benefits which can accrue to teachers and students from effective evaluation are sacrificed through its perverted use as a means of establishing and maintaining classroom control. This unfortunate practice continues in spite of the fact that the typical progress report clearly separates behavior from achievement. While there is sufficient documentation to support the theory that disruptive behavior reduces learning outcomes, this does not justify devaluating what has been learned effectively.

This indictment of the evaluation process should not be understood as a recommendation to return to the practices of the 60's. During that period, assessments of minority students' progress were inflated intentionally as a means of improving their self-concepts. That kind of intellectual dishonesty served no useful purpose in terms of improving motivation to achieve. However, it was instrumental in convincing educators that a more practical way to enhance students' self-images is to provide them with the skills needed to experience success. This can be accomplished without either inflating or deflating evaluations of their achievements. One of the things pointed out clearly by the research of the 70's is that those teachers who devise and implement effective systems for monitoring and providing feedback on students' achievement are the same teachers who produce significantly greater learning outcomes.

While the more effective teachers present students with increased opportunities for learning, their equation for effectiveness also reflects a set of expectations and attitudes that nurture learning. They believe that their students can learn anything which is taught effectively. If the curricular experiences, instructional strategies, or the feedback processes being employed are not producing the desired results, they find ways to modify them. In general, these teachers view student failure as a real challenge rather than consider certain groups of youngsters as being unteachable.

Popular misconceptions of the effects of pluralism on the education enterprise continue to cloud the issue of evaluation. M. Donald Thomas, superintendent of the Salt Lake City school district, presents some rather persuasive arguments against the concept of pluralism, and unwittingly against the movement toward equity for minorities. He maintains that:

- Pluralism eventually destroys any real sense of common traditions, values, purposes, and obligations . . . that schools lack unity and direction without such commonly supported positions.

- Pluralism in schools, at some point, makes it impossible for them to teach a common body of knowledge. It diverts schools' attention from their basic purpose of educating for civic, economic, and personal effectiveness.

- Pluralism in schools, at some point, tends to create moral anarchy. It lends support to the concept of no-fault morality which claims that all values are of equal worth and that the ends justify the means.[1]

If only a few superintendents adopt philosophies similar to that which Thomas has subscribed, the equity movement will be relegated to a position of pre-1954 significance.

Given the reality that schools are catering to culturally diverse populations, it is reasonable to assume that many students in attendance embrace perceptions, values, and customs which differ widely from those held by main-stream Americans. This recognition is a prerequisite for achieving unbiased evaluations. Toward that end, educators need to discover students' personal and ethnic strengths and avoid viewing cultural differences as deficits and disadvantages. If this philosophy is adopted by more educators, evaluation will become more valid and students' best interests are more likely to be served. In the section that follows, key ideas relating to more effective evaluation will be presented along with supportive rationale.

Toward More Effective Evaluation

Like many of the suggestions presented in this handbook, those that follow are not supported by extensive research findings. They are being offered because they are educationally sound and, more importantly, because they work.

1. Refrain From The Excessive Use Of Superlatives

The excessive use of superlatives such as super, fantastic, magnificent, and marvelous sends clear signals about teacher expectations for student performance. This, of course, assumes that those same superlatives are used consistently for performances which are qualitatively equivalent. Even if we accept that assumption as fact, there are undesirable consequences inherent in this practice which must not be overlooked. On the one hand, children who are recipients of such glowing comments are often led to believe that they have reached a level of proficiency which leaves little to be desired. While they usually maintain their present levels of academic performance, they are not easily motivated to extend themselves beyond those levels. On the other hand, there are many children assigned to most classes for whom the superlatives are clearly out of reach. The message to these children is that they can never perform in a manner expected by the teacher. As a result, they resign themselves to life in the slow lane and proceed to achieve accordingly.

This pitfall can be avoided by using comparative analyses in the evaluation process. By comparing present and past performances, skillful teachers can reward students for each successive approximation of what is desired. This can be accomplished without having students lose confidence in themselves or feel that they have reached maximum proficiency.

2. **Recognize The Problems Inherent In Summative Evaluations**

Summative evaluation techniques restrict assessment to learning outcomes and exclude the process by which those outcomes are produced. That indictment alone should be sufficient to call into question that unlimited use these techniques are receiving. However, rather than subsiding, their use is increasing in popularity. Even more distressing is the knowledge that this increase in use serves to perpetuate many ineffective teaching practices. The prevailing belief seems to be that when all students are presented with a body of information and given equal opportunity to learn, fairness demands that they be judged on the basis of competencies demonstrated. Accompanying this posture is the assumption that students' success or failure is determined entirely by their capacity for learning. This also suggests that neither the teachers nor the school should be held accountable for marginal or unsatisfactory student performances. Any decisions which follow from that kind of educational thought limit achievement for all students. Anything considered to be bad for students in general must be worse for minorities.

3. **Recognize The Benefits Of Formative Evaluation**

Standing in stark contrast to tests used for assessing achievement only are data collecting devices which provide information vital to the formation of learning experiences. Formative evaluation instruments are used:

a. To inform students about what they have learned.

b. To inform students about what they still need to learn.

c. To inform teachers about which learning experiences might need to be modified.

When feedback is provided regarding corrective needs and additional time and assistance are available, most students will reach a level of competence commensurate with their potential. What is being described here is essentially a cycle of assess, teach, reassess, and reteach. The intervening variables consist of adjustments in programs for students and adjustments by teachers in the delivery of instructional services. When used effectively, the data from formative evaluations ensure that most students demonstrate competence in the prerequisites necessary for each new learning task. As a result, students display greater confidence in their ability to learn, and spend more time actively engaged in the learning process. In short, students seem to become more proficient at learning how to learn, and teachers make more appropriate decisions about what to teach and how it can be taught most effectively.

4. Recognize The Danger Inherent In Combining Evaluations Of Academic Achievement And Behavior

Teachers who allow evaluation of academic performances to become a "smoking gun" for managing behavior are not only engaging in intellectual dishonesty, they are destroying students' motivation to achieve. It is conceivable that a student's behavior can get in the way of academic progress. However, what needs to be reflected in an evaluation of that progress is an honest assessment of achievement. In this case, behavior can and should be incorporated legitimately into the grade without damaging a teacher's integrity. On the other hand, there are literally thousands of students who perform flawlessly academically but are slapped with poor grades because of their behavior. Students who consistently cause grief for teacher are seldom rewarded with good grades. The point being made here is that it takes a special kind of person to resist the temptation of using the "smoking gun." However, effective teachers are very special people.

5. Recognize The Impact Of Oral Assessments

Teachers convey what they perceive as the value of students' contributions in many different ways. The manner through which they accept or reject those contributions influences how students will react to teacher expectations in the future. Remarks used for rejecting student responses run the gamut from mildly insensitive to grossly inappropriate. The lower end of that continuum contains "put downs" such as, "It's obvious you haven't read;" or "That makes no sense at all." Is it reasonable to assume that students will respond positively to such comments? Unfortunately, minorities are subjected to this more frequently than other students. Although the results are devastating, it continues to happen and few educators seem to be alarmed.

It is safe to conclude that evaluative statements and other comments made by teachers are seldom inconsequential. Those of us who can accept the premise that the ultimate purpose of evaluation is to assist in bringing about improvement should be striving to use it in that manner. To accomplish that end, evaluation must be honest, equitable, specific, and supportive.

[1] M. Donald Thomas, "The Limits of Pluralism," <u>Phi Delta Kappan</u>, LXII (April, 1981), 589-591.

Chapter VI

SOME FINAL COMMENTS

A major factor contributing to the lack of academic achievement for minorities is ineffective teaching. This is not an indictment against teaching in general, but rather its impact on particular groups. Minorities may be defined as those individuals or groups that possess traits, characteristics, and other lifeways which run counter to those of the dominant culture in our society. What schools have managed to accomplish for many of these students is nothing short of criminal. While it can be assumed that there has been no criminal intent, the results are no less devastating.

If minority students are ever to achieve at levels commensurate with their potential, then the efforts of educators must be directed toward controlling or, at least manipulating, those critical variables that influence learning. This strategy holds the potential for generating a tremendous amount of positive results from only a limited amount of educational reform. Its appeal and, ultimately, its success or failure rest on the recognition by educators that subtle adjustments in the delivery of instructional services to minorities can produce incredible gains in academic achievement.

Although the changes being recommended through this handbook are relatively minor, the process of changing teacher interactions with children is the major obstacle that must be overcome. More specifically, consciously determined as opposed to intuitively derived educational exchanges with youth are crucial to the successful manipulation of those critical variables. However, this kind of change can be facilitated through an awareness of the benefits which may be realized. That kind of awareness is increased when teachers:

1. Seek information about minority cultures from all available sources.

2. Verify the information obtained to form a knowledge base.

3. Develop from that knowledge base a set of understandings which serves to modify many current teaching behaviors.

Attempts to alleviate minority underachievement are compounded by the fact that schools, both public and private, are designed for middle-class white Americans. Combine that set of circumstances with the knowledge that many educators view the lack of achievement by minorities as a situation which will remain impervious to change and the odds against success are almost insurmountable. To subvert this blueprint for failure, scientifically controlled interventions by educators are essential.

Of the many variables associated with the teaching/learning equation, four emerge as critical in terms of their influence on education in general and education for minority students in particular. These critical variables are:

Motivation
Classroom Behavior
Student/Teacher Interaction
Evaluation

Motivation was examined from the perspective of two components which contribute toward its impact on learning:

1. Interest—Interest, as it is used here, relates to the students' need to know or perceived relevance of the learning task.

2. Transfer—Transfer is the process of bridging the gap between the learners' existing knowledge and the new learning task.

Creating interest and establishing positive transfer represent the most difficult challenges educators must face. Together, they form the contingencies upon which the success or failure of planned learning experiences rest. The need for educators to handle them successfully becomes THE FIRST AND GREAT COMMANDMENT! Their significance is acquired partially from the fact that they must occur at the very outset of a learning experience and partially from their power to influence all that follows.

Because of the time and effort required to create interest and establish positive transfer effectively, they are the most demanding aspects of the teaching endeavor. The difficulty encountered in accomplishing them successfully is directly related to the amount of cultural, ethnic, racial, and economic diversity present in any given classroom. Needless to say, the manner in which these variables have been handled for minority students leaves much to be desired.

Regardless of the amount of cultural diversity present, all of the students can learn the same skills. However, it is because they learn these same skills for a variety of different reasons that the responsibility for creating students' perceptions of relevance rests with the teacher. If the time and energy required to accomplish this effectively are not invested up front, then that investment must be directed toward managing behavior.

If we can accept the premise that disruptive behavior and on-task behavior are mutually exclusive, more time and energy will go into satisfying the requirements for creating positive attitudes toward learning and less in the direction of managing behavior. It is a well-established reality that behavior problems are minimized when teachers:

1. Create interest in the learning activity by having children perceive its relevance.

2. Establish positive transfer by relating the learning task to things the learners already know.

Since there are no guarantees that these two lesson components will be satisfied for each child present, and that if satisfied, non-task oriented behavior will be nonexistent, effective behavior management techniques were discussed.

It is clear that the conventional wisdom upon

which many teachers have come to rely for minimizing acceptable behavior is functionally obsolete. That obsolescence was brought on by the increases in cultural and ethnic diversity in many classroom settings. Again, the need for developing a set of understandings relating to minority cultures should be underscored. Those understandings emerge as constant reminders that our purpose for controlling behavior is to facilitate interactions that enhance learning. That purpose is best served by encouraging students to make appropriate choices between what is and what is not appropriate for school.

There is a causal relationship between student/ teacher interactions and learning outcomes. While there are many intervening variables, that complex relationship can be reduced to one simple fact. Any given interaction between teacher and student influences all subsequent interactions. This is why those interactions of teachers should represent consciously determined interventions. The manner in which far too many teachers handle disruptive behavior reduces significantly the prospects for subsequent meaningful interactions.

Because mutual respect is often destroyed by teacher acts of commission rather than acts of omission, emphasis was placed on those things that should not be done.

1. DON'T MORALIZE.

2. DON'T DEMEAN BEHAVIORS.

3. DON'T GET INTO POWER STRUGGLES.

4. DON'T IGNORE UNACCEPTABLE BEHAVIOR.

It is important to understand that most non-conforming behavior does not follow from students' desires to disregard school rules, but rather from the social structures from which reinforcement is derived. Teachers who recognize that fact direct their energies toward encouraging youth to make appropriate choices. Those who persist in defining classroom management as a campaign to eradicate those behaviors that assault their personal values are not only fighting a losing battle, they are erecting barriers that help render the primary mission of schooling ineffective.

Probably the most important thing to remember when dealing with inappropriate behavior is that the responsibility of educators is to help youth make choices based on a range of consequences. Teachers have no responsibility to teach the difference between what is morally "right" or "wrong."

Teaching, when reduced to its essence, may be thought of as interaction which induces learning. While learning can occur without the benefit of teaching, such learning is relatively inconsequential in terms of producing an educated citizenry. The more contemporary view of the educative process holds to the belief that its success or failure rests on the quality of the teaching.

For those who accept the notion that the quality control for the teaching/learning act is interaction, a frame of reference against which interaction may be judged is being provided. If all of these questions can be answered in the affirmative, students would have to be extremely ingenious not to learn.

An Anatomy Of Effective Teaching

1. Did the lesson introduction include:

   a) A brief period of recall?

   b) Strategies designed to stimulate interest?

   c) Strategies designed to establish positive transfer?

   d) Clear teacher expectations for student performance?

2. Did the delivery of instructional services include:

   a) A blend of lecture, demonstration, and active student participation?

   b) Strategies designed to stimulate both left and right-brain functioning? (logical and sequential as well as spatial and holistic)

   c) Strategies designed to facilitate students' learning from other students? (cooperative learning techniques)

   d) Questioning techniques that stimulated literal, interpretative, critical, and creative thought processes?

   e) Strategies that complimented a variety of learning styles? (visual, auditory, tactile, and kinesthetic)

f) Active teaching attention being directed toward each student present?

g) Immediate feedback to reinforce acceptable and encourage remediation of unacceptable responses?

h) The use of EPR techniques? (Every Pupil Response)

i) Appropriate use of teacher wait time?

j) Appropriate strategies for accepting or rejecting student responses?

k) Behavior management techniques which were humanly enhancing and mutually rewarding?

l) Opportunities for the practical application of skills taught?

m) The cycle of assess, teach, evaluate, and reteach?

3. Did the lesson closure include:

a) Utilization of both formative and summative evaluation techniques?

b) Suggestions for subsequent lessons from both students and teacher?

4. Did the learning environment reflect:

   a) An atmosphere in which mutual respect was established and maintained?

   b) An atmosphere in which risk taking was encouraged?

Teachers who consistently perform at the conscious level can isolate and examine each of these behaviors for its impact on the learning process. This kind of introspection is extremely useful in identifying those behaviors which generate the most favorable results.

Pareto, the Italian economist and sociologist, achieved a measure of prominence for applying principles of economics to social interaction. His analysis of the economy of effort expended on a variety of human endeavors gave rise to the 80-20 rule. This rule states that 80% of the accomplishments realized from most human interactions results from only 20% of the effort invested. A commitment from educators to identify and improve that 20% which has contributed to minority achievement in the past would improve significantly their chances for success in the future.

Evaluation, the final variable, must be considered as a strategy for improving both the process and the product of the school experience. If it accomplishes one but not the other, it becomes suspect. However, if it accomplishes neither, it should be abandoned completely.

Given the reality that schools are catering to culturally diverse populations, teachers must realize that many of their students will embrace perceptions, values, and customs which differ from those held by main-stream Americans. This realization is a prerequisite to unbiased evaluations.

One of the more serious indictments against evaluation is that it often reflects teacher perceptions of student behavior as well as achievement. This notion is supported by the fact that boys usually score higher than girls on tests of math and science, yet girls receive better grades than boys in these same subjects on report cards. Evaluation of minority students' work suffers even greater contamination because these children behave in ways that are different from middle-class students. Many teachers see these behaviors not only as unacceptable but limiting in terms of academic growth.

The discussion of behavior management pointed out that many teachers are ill-equipped to deal effectively with behaviors that present disruptions to normal classroom activities. Teacher frustrations arising from feelings of not being in control are vented through the process of evaluating student achievement. The most academically able students who cause management problems for teachers are likely to receive poor grades.

Minority students are victimized not only by being taught ineffectively, but by being labeled learning disabled for their lack of achievement. Many school systems continue to use the discrepancy between ability and achievement as an indicator of some kind of learning problem. This practice, when used exclusively, completely disregards the clear distinction that can and should be made between students who are knowledge deficient and those who exhibit some type of cognitive dysfunction.

Obviously, controlling the four variables presented in this handbook cannot guarantee that all minority students will achieve at levels commensurate with their abilities. However, if educators utilize these strategies as a means toward that end, they will have taken a giant step in the right direction.

BIBLIOGRAPHY

Arnez, N.L. "Implications of Desegregation as a Discriminatory Process," Journal of Negro Education, XLVII (1978), 28-45.

Bloom, Benjamin S. "The New Direction in Educational Research: Alterable Variables," Phi Delta Kappan, LXI (February, 1980), 382-385.

Bloom, Benjamin S. "Talent Development vs. Schooling," Educational Leadership, XXXIX (November 1981), 86-94.

Brown, Thomas J. and Orland Taylor "Should Black English Be Taught in the Elementary Schools?" Instructor, LXXXIX (April, 1980), 22.

Crain, R. L., and R. Mahard. "Desgregation and Black Achievement: A Review of the Research," Law and Comtemporary Problems, XLLI (1978), 17-56.

Crain, R. L., and R. Mahard. "Some Policy Implications of the Desegregation Minority Achievement Literature," In Hawley, W. D. ed., Assessment of Current Knowledge About the Effectiveness of School Desegregation Strategies. Nashville, Tennessee: Vanderbilt University,

Institute for Public Policy Studies, Center for Education and Human Development, 1981.

Crowl, T.K., "White Teachers' Evaluation of Oral Responses Given by White and Negro Ninth Grade Males, "Dissertation Abstracts, 3, (1971: 4540A.)

Edelman, M. W. Portrait of Inequality: Black and White Children in America. Washington, D.C.: Washington Research Project, 1980.

Epps, E. C. Cultural Pluralism. California: McCutchan Publishing Corporation, 1974.

Epps, E. C. "The Impact of School Desgregation on the Self-Evaluation and Achievement Orientation of Minority Children," Law and Contemporary Problems, XLII (Summer, 1978), 57-76.

Finley, David "Why Eskimo Education Isn't Working," Phi Delta Kappan, LXIV (April, 1983), 580-581.

Good, T. L. "Teacher Expectations and Student Perceptions: A Decade of Research," Educational Leadership XXXVIII (April, 1981): 415-422.

Good, T. L., and J. E. Brophy. "Analyzing Classroom Interactions: A More Powerful Alternative," Educational Technology, XI (October, 1971), 36.

Hale, Janice E. Black Children: Their Roots, Culture and Learning Styles New York: Brigham, 1982.

Hall, L. "Race and Suspension; A Second General Desegregation Problem," In Moody C.D., J. William, and C.B. Vergen ed., Student Rights and Discipline. Ann Arbor, Michigan: University of Michigan School of Law, 1978.

Leacock, Eleanor. Teaching and Learning in City Schools: A Comparative Study. New York: Basic Books, 1969.

Rist, R. C. "Student Social Class and Teacher Expectation: The Self-fulfilling Prophecy in Ghetto Education," Harcard Educational Review, XL (1970), 411-415.

Rubovitz, P. C., and M. Maehr. "Pygmalion Black and White," Journal of Personality and Social Psychology, XXV (1973), 210.

Smith, G. Pritchy. "The Critical Issue of Excvellence and Equity in Competency Testing," Journal of Teacher Education, XXXV (March-April, 1984), 6-9.

Stodolsky, Susan, and Gerald Lesser. "Learning Patterns in the Disadvantaged," Harvard Educational Review, XXXVII (Fall, 1967), 546-593.

Thomas, M. Donald "The Limits of Pluralism," Phi Delta Kappan, LXII (April, 1981), 589-591.

Woodworth, W.P., and Salzer, R.T., "Black Children's Speech and Teacher Evaluations," Urban Education, VI (July, 1971), 167-173.